Fundamentals of Computer Network Analysis and Engineering

Fundamentals of Computer Network Analysis and Engineering

■

Basic approaches for solving
problems in the networked
computing environment

J. Radz

iUniverse, Inc.
New York Lincoln Shanghai

Fundamentals of Computer Network Analysis and Engineering
Basic approaches for solving problems in the networked computing environment

Copyright © 2005 by J. Radz

iUniverse books may be ordered through booksellers or by contacting:

iUniverse
2021 Pine Lake Road, Suite 100
Lincoln, NE 68512
www.iuniverse.com
1-800-Authors (1-800-288-4677)

ISBN-13: 978-0-595-37670-4 (pbk)
ISBN-13: 978-0-595-82054-2 (ebk)
ISBN-10: 0-595-37670-3 (pbk)
ISBN-10: 0-595-82054-9 (ebk)

Printed in the United States of America

Contents

Author's note

Work on this book started in the year 2000. I had originally intended to publish a book that visited all the 'iconic' stages of an idea toward a solution. The first page of a chapter would be a sketch on a napkin and the last a polished diagram of a completed system. I had stacks upon stacks of these drawings. Looking through the stacks, I realized that the drawings by themselves would have little value to another individual; it was the method of progressing from the napkin to the completed diagram that I actually wished to convey.

I began exploring this progressive method. I realized that my stacks of drawings represented a definite fundamental approach to administration and engineering.

It took me over a year of late nights to complete, but what resulted from my effort was a simple foundational approach to computer network administration and engineering; it was easy to view much like the original drawings I intended to use. I tried to exclude reference to modern technologies, description of current scenarios, Internet addresses, and other time-sensitive information (things that may have no applicability to a future computing environment). In 2001, I believed that I had a completed book and that the fundamentals contained inside could be applied to any networked computing environment—past, present, and future.

My own scope of responsibility widened, largely due to application of the guidelines; they had proved themselves in battle time and time again to result in success and lead to further exploration. My focus on career impacted the delivery of this text to the public, and although I practiced these methods daily the fact that I had them in writing eventually left my mind and this book was shelved along with the stacks of drawings on napkins.

For several years I maintained an intense focus on my practice, naturally applying my own methods, which I believed to be correct. I continued to observe individuals and groups who were dealing with highly detailed and complex initiatives while ignoring elementary rules, the very principles from which technology itself was birthed. I noted that the longer these principles were ignored the more they were needed to resolve issues that spawned by that disregard. I found myself continually trying to communicate these ideas through analogies, which seemed to have the highest degree of success above other delivery methods. But retention was a problem; these principles, as elementary as they are, were often given a lower value than implementing quick fixes and saving time.

I found myself thinking: What if individuals had a reference that was easy to read; a reference that could quickly refresh, through simple analogies, the core ideas that are the foundation of technical work? What if focus could be placed on the fundamentals alone? Then I recalled the disk buried under the stacks of paper from years ago.

Wait, I already have this.

I make no apologies for the relatively low quantity of words in these writings. The analogies and approaches contained here are fundamental (thus the title *Fundamentals of Computer Network Analysis and Engineering*); they are basic principles and not technical overviews—technical manuals such as those just mentioned are readily available from other sources.

That being stated (what this book does not provide), what this book will provide is a basic approach to learning through observation, keeping record of what is learned (the drawings mentioned previously), and using that record to retain, refresh, and share the education gained. It also provides insight into using the intimacy achieved to formulate and solve problems at the highest (or lowest, depending on the perspective) level; how to *build with blocks* if you will.

I feel strongly about the importance of these principles. I even believe they have applicability to areas outside networked computing environments.

1

the objective of definition

In some computing environments, network engineers have grown their practices from seeds of imaginative concepts and mysterious administrative legends. Administration or engineering based on these nonspecific ideas will shape a computing environment into a fact less domain and will also make analysis from within that domain seemingly impossible. The formulation of problems and the solutions to those problems must be the result of tactical fact assembly and analysis; every component, every factor, and every subsystem should be known by measurement and not by guesswork. Although concepts have great value as starting points for realizing a design, or as a placeholder or mark for further exploration, they should not be the only consideration when inventing a solution, but rather the starting point and only the starting point; the starting point for ongoing factual discovery or magnification.

A specialist should not be defined as one who possesses a set of instructions or reference material written by another individual, or one who has direct and quick access to said material, but as one who has the ability to create reference material from the ground up based personal knowledge and experience. Several methods for measuring and recording the scope and detail of a computing environment should be applied, including the use of logical determination where physical measurements are not immediately possible. One method should cross the other wherever possible to verify the validity of the method itself. These measurements are used to maintain the critical perspective of the whole environment.

The network specialist should explore the function of information collection and also the application of these discoveries to a physical medium, such as paper or models represented in a single dimension or multiple dimensions. Use of various methods will be required to accomplish this, and the differences between physical and logical mapping should be known and each method practiced.

These basic practices should be applied to all subsystems in the networked computing environment, from the core network infrastructure down to the handheld computer.

A network engineer should not be continually dealing with computing disasters. If disasters are commonplace, this is an indicator that a total perspective must be achieved and a design change must take place. Through the changes in design, intimacy will be achieved. Where intimacy exists, potential for specific disasters are identified and that potential can be removed.

Every engineer faced with a wrecked environment should not be hesitant to use elementary mathematics and basic models to begin solving the problem: How do I restore the environment? Simple formulas are of course the foundation for more complex formulas and so on. If the result of the current master equation equals 'wrecked' then one cannot argue with the logic that it must be disassembled and reassembled.

Identification, the first step in reinventing the wrecked environment, is the process of eliminating the unknown, or making the unknown known. During this process, gray areas are either given an actual value or marked to indicate that a real value is needed.

Bad: Language such as 'bad' has nested itself deep into the operational history of computer network administration as a perfectly acceptable reason for failure of a system or subsystem. The terms 'bad' and 'good' by themselves define nothing specific, factual, or real. Both the result that is desired (good) and the result that is not desired (bad) must be defined.

Stuff: What is 'stuff'? Stuff always boils to specific components, processes or factors. If there is a pile of stuff, what is in that pile? 'The smell is coming from that pile of stuff,' even though there is only one offending item. That single item has a potential for affecting the rest of the pile. If it is not identified, the pile becomes ruined.

Corrupt: Corruption is the result of immeasurable modifiers. Where this term is applicable is in communications to parties that do not have the capacity, either in knowledge or time, to digest all factors that equal the state. 'The government of country Z is corrupt.' Is it necessary to list every angle of corruption and all contributors to get the point across? An engineer should, however, have the capacity and the time to know these factors; their job may be to communicate the state of the environment, but above that is the responsibility to remove the 'corruption.' In fact, to design or redesign an environment that is resistant to negative states, an identification of these variables and their current values is critical. Their representation on a physical map is also critical.

Something: The word something really means nothing. It means a thing that has not been identified. What thing is it? This question is the first question to be answered in any effort.

2

the basic principle of gradual magnification

Using simple methods applied with precision, any individual can successfully comprehend even the most complex computing environments.

Before administering any environment, it must be identified in total. What specifically are the components that equal the total environment and how do they relate to one another? Who uses the environment and how are these 'users' classed?

There will always be factors that cannot be initially realized because they exist beyond the immediate senses; they cannot be seen, but they are known to exist through other indicators, commonly an operational environment. These can be physical items, such as microprocessors in a computer or cables under a floor. They can also be nonphysical factors, such as network protocol. Representing these things on a diagram allows one to see what they are dealing with when dealing with physically hidden factors that are in fact critical organs in a networked system.

Only after measurements have been taken can analysis begin. For a proper analysis to take place, the whole territory must be considered. In a networked computing environment, one component or factor can, and often does, affect the entire environment. Only after a complete view is assembled can these relationships be understood.

Would you attempt to map a road that you have not yet traveled? If you are lost and find yourself traveling down the same road repeatedly, would you not start mapping the area as you travel so you can determine the next logical direction you should take?

As territory is explored, understanding of the environment naturally increases and depth is added to the maps. Great insight is gained into the environment while the map is being drawn.

To add territory to the map with no evidence of said territory is certain to equal disaster; that is, every addition to the map must be based some type of understanding, even if that understanding is at the most basic level. If you were lost, you would not invent areas where absolutely no evidence of these areas existed.

A *temporary* substitute can be used in place of an actual physical measurement, but it cannot be solely imaginative; it must be an *educated* guess based on what is known; this is a placeholder that must be expanded on as understanding is increased.

The following is a far-reaching example that serves the purpose of demonstrating this concept well: It was once said that the moon was made of green cheese. As nonsensical as that sounds based on our current knowledge of the moon's composition, the moon is in fact more like green cheese than it is like a ball of fire. The moon has a type of bland color, maybe not green, but certainly more green than red or purple. The surface of the moon is not smooth, like that of refined marble, and does in fact have the appearance of some types of cheese. Further scientific studies of the moon have revealed that it is not in fact made of cheese. It was not truly until physical study (actual measurement) that it could be determined without a doubt that the moon was not composed of cheese. It was during this process that green cheese could be removed from the maps and replaced with specific types of rock. The important thing to note in this example is that further understanding of the moon's composition was desired, and through great and detailed efforts, finally obtained.

By first representing the moon as green cheese (versus not representing it at all), it created a starting point or an area to be expanded upon. In the case of the moon and the green cheese it was originally thought to consist of, the argument that it was a large ball of cheese floating in space was weak at best; but as mentioned before it is suitable for example purposes. In fact, this example in itself is a placeholder of sorts for the future use of more advanced discovery methods that are, at the core, similar in design.

The following diagrams demonstrate the concept of adding depth to a physical record of an environment. There are two squares in the following diagrams. Each black square represents the same whole environment. Diagram (A) represents the environment where three subsystems (defined as functionally related components) are known and mapped. Diagram (A) is an example of relatively simple understanding of the target environment—underlying subsystems exist but have not been discovered and are not known. As the need for further examination arises, *as it will* through the natural course of observation, more subsystems that contribute to the environment become evident. Upon their discovery, through research and other processes, they are added to the map. Resulting maps reflect a higher understanding of the environment, or diagram (B).

A

B

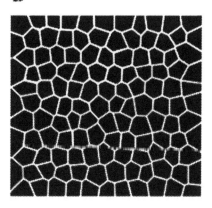

Consider how the moon's surface, as used in a previous example, is recorded at three relatively lower and higher levels of understanding. The lowest level of understanding is green cheese; in other words, the moon is known to exist but nothing beyond the fact that it has a surface is known (a black square). An increased level of understanding is where actual types of rock are known. An even higher level of understanding is knowledge of rock types and knowledge of the location of specific rocks on the moon's surface. The expert or specialist in this example would have records (maps) of rock types and locations based on identification and discovery, and the same records would reflect the elements that equaled each individual rock type, based on analysis.

How are the locations of specific areas of rock and the physical properties of the rocks obtained? Physically traveling to the surface in a spacecraft and directly observing the environment, or remotely using fact-gathering tools such as a telescope or a probe accomplishes this.

3

discovering the territory

A physical discovery is when components such as cables, switches, servers, and software are observed directly.

A logical discovery involves obtaining evidence that a component *must* exist and also involves obtaining the properties of that component, even though it cannot be directly observed.

The physically discovered component is that which is directly observed, such as a group of workstations in a room that the specialist has entered, a communications hub in the same room, and cabling that connects the workstations to the hub and the hub to a wall receptacle.

Where distance between physical components or other limitations are present, and those limitations prevent immediate physical discovery (the vastness of space), a logical method of discovery is used. Components that are not directly accessible for physical identification can be discovered using programs that touch or trace a path to these components (ex: PING, Traceroute). Once the pencil lines have been drawn, other utilities (ex: Telnet) can be used to connect to the devices to obtain more details.

The most challenging environments to chart are those that were not designed by the person or team responsible for them. These are *inherited environments*. In addition to being designed by another individual or group, inherited environments may also have been administered by a separate individual our group of individuals who were not responsible for the design.

Before the specialist lies the environment or an idea of a new environment. Some factors are known and other factors are unknown. The problem is: Where to start? Obtaining a stronghold on an initial component or subsystem is the first step; where to place that grip is decided by answering the following question, which is opposite of the original problem (how to make the unknown known).

The question is: What is known? If nothing is known, then the question is: What is easiest to assimilate? In a networked computing environment each subsystem relates to every other. If one of those relationships is used to begin a discovery process, other relationships will also be discovered, as opposed to an unfocused approach where subsystems are identified at random.

For the new environment being designed the grip must be placed on a future component, or the green cheese. The need is for clients to share files; a file server is required. The file server is the starting point. An inward or outward approach can be used. A workstation for the user [to access the file server] is required and could also be the starting point. The properties of these components are not yet known but can be represented on a map with detail added at a later time when the actual properties are known (green cheese to rock).

In most cases, more than one component will be immediately known. Even though a starting point has been established, this does not mean that other known components cannot be added to the map. Consider an environment with four components: A, B, C, and D. *A* is the starting point, B and C have not been proved to exist, and D is known. Components A and D can be added to the map. For this example, A is a workstation and D is a file server. Because it is obvious by basic analysis of the workstation that there is a connection (or needed connection in the case of the environment being designed) or communications channel between A and D, proof of other components already exists with no further study. One only needs to determine what the properties of these components are. Using logical discovery, these components can be identified and the map updated. A level of understanding is then established, a level which can then be increased (rock to types of rock).

Similarities between components will become apparent during discovery. The process of differencing can be used to quickly assimilate components with similar properties or function. Example: In an office there is a single file server that houses files shared by users of fifty workstations. If the discovery is focused on a single workstation, and that discovery is very detailed, the subsequent forty-nine discoveries become only a matter of calculating the difference between the *control* (workstation 1) and the remainder (workstations 2-49).

Differencing is an important skill. The application of differencing goes beyond what is obviously similar; in the example workstations are of course similar in both purpose and basic design, but do other components share properties?

Differencing can be used to assimilate new technologies that share the same core design as technologies of the past. One who has a great deal of insight into the workstation that is twenty years old can draw lines between what is known about the old and what remains with the new. In most cases, drawing these parallels eliminates the bulk of discovery work—there is no need to revisit or reconsider factors that have not changed.

4

introduction to positive and negative states

Providing that maps are accurate, a positive state should be easily recognized: No reports from 'listeners' or users, no alerts, no errors in logs, no thresholds exceeded, and no unexpected results according to the design that is directly reflected on the map. As intimacy increases with ongoing analysis (what should take place while a positive state is present), the result will be an increased understanding of the environment which will in turn result in more detailed maps, which will ultimately lead to more in depth analysis.

If the engineer and the specialist are the same individual and a controlled approach was taken when implementing a new design or re engineering the environment (including updates to the map), then a negative state should easily be detected.

If the engineer or specialist had no previous interest in the environment (the environment was inherited), it can be assumed that the maps are not accurate and that it may be difficult to maintain or even determine the state of the environment.

A *condition* is defined as a thing that limits, restricts, or modifies another thing. A positive system can be modified by a negative condition and a negative system can be modified by a positive condition.

A positive state is present in a system or subsystem when the sum of *positive* conditions relative in that system is equal to the number of actual conditions. In the simplest terms, if all conditions are positive then the state of the environment is positive.

A negative state is present when a positive environment is modified by any negative condition, the operative word being *modified*. A notable difference between a positive state and a negative state is that the presence of a single negative condition in a positive state changes the whole positive state to negative; a single positive condition present in a negative state does not necessarily change the negative state to positive.

Unknown states are those where the state is not known to be either negative or positive, even when observation is taking place. An unknown state is evidence that further identification is needed; that the depth of discovery is less than what is required by observation. Therefore, an unknown state is a negative state by default.

5

the goal of observation

The environment as charted should be continually observed, or *monitored*, to confirm a positive state or detect a negative state. Results will simply be positive (by design), negative, or unknown (not understood). Monitoring is only used to determine if the state of the environment is positive, negative, or unknown. Problem solving is the next logical step after the state has been determined.

An indication of a negative state could arrive in an electronic mail or voice communication from a user or users of the environment. Alerts received from monitoring tools, configured to advise administrators of modified states may indicate a negative state. Indicators such as those mentioned must be verified. Verifying the validity of indicators is also part of the monitoring process.

There are several monitoring methods. The first is the physical or direct method; this is a method that can be applied to the part of the environment that is physically available, or can be directly viewed or manipulated. A computer in open view would be an example of a component that could be physically monitored. Connecting to a system using modems or via the Internet is also considered an application of a direct or physical monitoring process.

The primary advantage of the physical or direct method is accuracy. Monitoring the environment by checking logs, running tasks for which the system was designed (putting the environment through normal cycles), or running diagnostic routines will immediately reveal a negative, positive, or unknown state. Again, the desired result of monitoring the environment is not to determine *why* a state is negative or how to classify an unknown state as positive or negative, but only to determine *if* it is negative, positive, or unknown.

Of course, physically monitoring the environment at all times is impossible. There are tools available that automate the processes of watching event logs, running diagnostics against the target environment, and other monitoring tasks.

The advantage of tool use is clear and solves the problem, How do I monitor the environment when physical monitoring is not possible? Where the scope of physically monitoring all components and the whole environment is too large—and it will be in most cases—the implementation of automated monitoring supports the whole monitoring process and fills the gap.

Of course, every method has a disadvantage; and with tools that automate the process, there are some. When new tools are implemented for monitoring the environment, a new subsystem is then present, as these types of tools always include systems and programs that are linked to the environment. A positive state must also be maintained in the new subsystem (the monitoring subsystem), and implementing a monitoring subsystem in an existing environment can change the state of that environment from positive to negative.

The method of listening to the environment is that of translating communications from the environment itself, or listening for other indicators of a modified positive state. Sometimes these communications are subtle; sometimes they are hidden within other communications. This is always a good supplement to another method, but is usually not sufficient as the only method of effective monitoring. The practice of 'listening' is enhanced as a method is practiced, that is: with increased familiarity or clarity comes increased reception to these communications.

6

reinventing the wheel or the drawing of the wheel

Reinvention does not always mean or involve physically changing an environment. Reinvention can be, and often is, nothing more than a discovery or rediscovery of existing components in the environment, which until said discovery were not fully realized by the engineer. In other words, the environment may already be optimally configured but the configuration is not *known* to be optimal. This is most commonly found in the inherited environments and unknown states that were mentioned previously. In these cases, what is actually being reinvented is the map, *not the physical environment.* There must be a clear relationship between the map and the environment; if they are not reflections of one another then the maps must be updated. At least, the map must be accurate before any modification to the environment takes place.

If, based on discovery, analysis, and study of the accurate map an unidentifiable condition persists and a revelation is not obtained, reinvention is needed.

If there is an area of the map that is not understood, and the specialist is responsible for that area, said area must be analyzed until understood or physically changed so that the materials can be worked with. This may mean physical rearrangement, adjustment, or even removal of components.

Due to the large number of factors that contribute to a computing environment, a measurable number of components may be represented logically on the map throughout the life of the environment. But by looking at the map, the specialist should be able to say: This is how I understand this to work and the result confirms that understanding.

7

the potential dimensions of the map

In the First World War, paper battlefield maps were used to record plans of attack. Often these were gray maps of the terrain, with bold-colored ink marking the actual battle plan. The markings were clean stamps and lines that indicated the placement and direction of groups, the dates that these groups would be engaged, the path they would follow, and location of reserves. The markings on the maps stood out but did not completely obstruct the names of cities, countries, or railroads on the map. Any war strategist could determine by study of these maps what types of attacks would take place, when they would take place, and what physical materials (infantry, etc.) would be used.

Important to note is that actions, or statements of the things to be done, coexisted with the terrain on the map. Times, or schedules, were represented on the map. It was a total view of both the playing field and the game itself.

Another perspective on map dimensions can be gained from the incidents that occurred aboard the Apollo 13 spacecraft in 1970 during a mission to the moon's surface. An 'undervolt' condition on one of two main power circuits led to a series of problem-solving events, the solutions to which prevented human disaster and allowed the safe return of three astronauts. Unsolved, these open problems would have prevented their safe return.

One situation involved a three-dimensional map that would be directly used to apply the solution to one problem (there were several).

After a series of component failures, the astronauts did not have enough breathable air in the Lunar Module (LM) for the entire return trip home due to damage to critical subsystems in the Command Module (CM), which was attached to the LM.

Lithium hydroxide cartridges in the LM, which remove carbon dioxide from the air in the spacecraft, would only last about half of the journey home. Similar cartridges existed in the CM, but they would not fit the LM. The problem was—How could the CM cartridges be used in the LM, effectively extending the time that a breathable atmosphere would be present in the LM beyond the time it would take to return to Earth?

Ground engineers and astronauts, knowing the material the astronauts in space had to work with [on board the LM] created a three-dimensional model, or prototype, of an adapter that would allow use of the CM cartridges in the LM. Using the physical model, they were able to voice instructions for re-creating the adapter on board the spacecraft. They worked from their own map to implement the solution. Why would the inventors of the prototype need a prototype to relay ideas and instructions to the astronauts in space? Why couldn't they just relay the instructions directly? Because the engineers knew that a focus was needed and recalling their design (even though capable) every time an instruction was to be relayed was not efficient. An investment was made in the creation of the map—the master reference point. If changes to the design were needed, the map would be the first thing modified; in this scenario, only after the prototype was complete would the solution be implemented. If reinvention were needed, changes would first be made to the prototype. This prototype would directly reflect the adapter ultimately applied to the spacecraft. A comparison in pictures of the adapter on the LM and the prototype built by engineers shows this reflection.

8

isolation

The process of determining the root cause is commonly known as troubleshooting. Use of the phrase 'root cause' over the word 'troubleshooting' has been chosen here to stress use of the word *root*. When used in 'computer' terms, root is at the top of any hierarchy or chain, whether it is a directory tree or level of access. The word *shooting* also implies a hit-or-miss approach to solving problems, which is not needed if the territory is understood.

The tree serves as one half of an analogy comparing a failure in its system to that of a failure in a computing environment.

On this tree, some of the leaves are brown, and only green leaves are desired. Although the brown leaves can be removed from the tree, without water the remainder of leaves will eventually turn. By removing the brown leaves, only the conditions (symptoms) are being removed. The tree needs water, which is the root cause of the negative state.

Many specialists fail to dig through the earth, identify the system as a whole, see the roots and understand their purpose, and provide the tree with water.

Once the tree has been provided with water at the roots, the brown leaves can be removed. The environment is documented based on what has been learned. If brown leaves appear in the future, one only needs to look at the map to determine where to add water; the process of adding water is represented on the maps (battle plans). An engineer studying the map may decide to install a watering subsystem, and by study of the map would know where to place said subsystem.

Correcting or reversing a failure does not prevent future failures; only after determining the true root of the problem can preventative measures be enabled.

Maps help isolate subsystems, such as the tree root system in the aforementioned example. If more detailed views do not exist, the engineer will be presented with an opportunity to add that detail to this area of the map. During this fact gathering and magnification of the isolated subsystem (the dig for roots), a contributing factor or factors may be identified.

How, in environments more complex than the tree, are subsystems isolated?

In the following example, complex is defined as fifty subsystems where the relationship between the subsystems and the trouble system is unknown.

A ceiling-mounted light fixture has an inoperable switch. The switch is in a permanently closed position so the light remains on. In this scenario, the root cause is known but the problem is not solved, the whole problem being—how can the switch be repaired without injury to the person repairing it?

Examination of the breaker box reveals that the technician who installed the panel did not mark what breaker enables or disables what circuit (this is an inherited environment). It is known that the power to the light fixture must be disabled for any repair to take place. Which of the fifty breakers will disable the circuit specific to the light fixture so it can be repaired?

Here lies the opportunity for creating an accurate map of the subsystem (the specific circuit on which the light fixture exists). How is this isolated? By reducing the total number of subsystems in halves until the subsystem is identified.

Twenty-five (numbers 1-25) of the fifty breakers are moved to the 'off' position. The 'always on' light with the inoperable switch goes out when this action is taken. This means that the breaker linked to the light fixture must be in the range of 1-25. There is no need at this time to explore 26-50.

The twenty-five breakers are returned to the on position, restoring the environment to the original state—power is again being supplied to the fixture. Half (1-13) of the original half (1-25) are moved to the off position. The light does not go out; meaning one of the breakers in the range of 14-25 is linked to the trouble area. Switches 1-13 are returned to their original position.

Breakers 14-19 are moved to the off position and the light goes out. The range is now known to be 14-19, or one of six. The six is divided in half by turning 14-16 on. The light does not go back on, meaning breaker 17, 18, or 19, all still in the off position, is linked to the light and fixture. Seventeen and 18 are turned on and the light goes on, ruling out 19, which is returned to its original position as it has been ruled out. Seventeen is turned off and the light goes off. The breaker switch seventeen is linked to the light and fixture; at this point the subsystem has been isolated to one of fifty circuits.

During this exercise, if other circuits were monitored as the switches were moved between on and off, some relationships not directly related to the trouble could be identified.

When breaker switch nineteen was the only switch in the off position, what subsystems were affected? The repair person noted that the bedroom lights were also disabled when this switch was off. What other outlets or devices share the circuit with the light fixture related to breaker seventeen?

9

research

Bruce Lee, who was well known for his films, physique, and hand-to-hand combat techniques, was a pioneer in a special method of research toward solving a problem.

Mr. Lee's problem was this: How can I be effective in combat against any type of fighter? He considered the advantages of all known methods of combat: wrestling, boxing, street fighting, and many Eastern methods. His method of determining what the all-situation combat system and associated physique would be to gather information on all types of fighters (possible combaters and combatants), tear articles from magazines, and collect photographs of different fighter physiques. Bruce took all the gathered information and discarded all information not relevant to his goal. Select information from *each fighting style* was complied into what would become the solution to his problem, narrowing the view to his goal.

There is no doubt that during his research, Bruce encountered many bits of information that were not relevant to his problem. In all likelihood, he also encountered information that was not *directly* relevant to his problem but lead to information that was.

Could a man study only the techniques of a boxer and survive in combat against any type of fighter? Probably not; but he might borrow the footwork techniques of a boxer and combine them with the grappling techniques of a wrestler, increasing his chances of survival by a measurable amount.

Unfortunately, a common practice in problem solving is to apply solutions described in the first or second piece of information found when researching. This is usually because the desire of the engineer is to quickly solve the problem, rather than understand the area of the environment that is not understood—the reason for research in the first place—and repair it permanently.

Bruce Lee considered all material related to his goal, which had the potential to be both relevant and irrelevant. If during his research the first thing he encountered was an article on the upper arm strength of boxers, he would not have stopped there; if he lived in the modern age, he might use combinations such as *arm strength* and *upper arm* at the root of his search. Bruce may have even considered the exercise methods and techniques of a weightlifter, even though a weightlifter is not always a hand-to-hand combatant.

10

a short definition of problem

A dictionary lists more than one definition for the word problem:

1. A question raised for inquiry, consideration, or solution; a proposition in mathematics or physics stating something to be done.

2. A source of perplexity, distress, or vexation; difficulty in understanding or accepting.

It is true that a source of distress can be defined as a problem, but note that this definition also includes terms such as 'difficulty in understanding' and 'vexation'.

As a result of identification and isolation there should be more than adequate understanding of contributing factors, negating the value of 'difficulty in understanding' in one definition of the word problem. To formulate a problem is to translate an objective into a question. Objective: A functional repair switch; Problem: How is it repaired? The matter of solving the problem is then only a matter of answering the question. In a previous example, there was a problem: 'How can the CM cartridges be used in the LM, effectively extending the time that a breathable atmosphere would be present in the LM, beyond the time it would take to return to Earth?' The solution was the answer to that question.

11

the fly and the scientific method

An important perspective on the scientific method can be obtained from David Cronenberg's 1986 film adaptation of *The Fly*.

The film centered on the scientific exploits of Seth Brundle. Brundle was an inventor and a scientist who had designed the world's first teleportation system, which consisted of individual 'telepods'—a sending pod and a receiving pod. An object was placed into the sending telepod (point A), disassembled by the system at the molecular level, and reassembled within the receiving telepod (point B). The significance and impact of this invention is mentioned in the film but is not important here. What is important is the lesson learned when control is not observed.

Brundle had kept his telepod invention a secret until meeting a journalist with a scientific background; this journalist was very interested in the system, after Brundle had convinced her of its realness, but learned that Brundle had not yet determined how to send living objects from telepod to telepod without destroying the organisms completely upon reassembly. Together they engaged in a series of experiments to determine why this was not possible, and after some modifications to the system based on the results, Brundle was ready to transport a baboon from point A to point B.

The results were positive; the baboon was transported from point A to point B completely intact.

Seth then decided to transport himself from point to point without further analysis. The baboon appeared completely unaffected and indifferent after being transported from point A to B. The baboon appeared normal. Based on the result of his experiment there could be no other factors to consider. Making this assumption was Brundle's critical mistake—he assumed his single experiment included all possible factors.

Brundle began the sequence and stepped into his transportation environment. Emerging at point B, he, like the baboon, appeared normal. He uttered the comment 'Is it live or is it Memorex?'

At the time of his exit from the transporter, the answer to his question was unknown.

The turning point of the story is when the journalist asks the question 'You went through, without sending the baboon out for tests?' It is at this point in the film when it is realized, by Brundle and by the audience, that perhaps there were other possible factors to consider; that a hidden condition could have been present at the time of his transportation; that the transportation process was more complex than it appeared. The seriousness of Brundle's spontaneity is emphasized when the question is asked; and the importance of a scientific method begins to surface at that moment.

Unknown to Brundle, there was a fly in the sending chamber. Both the fly and Brundle were disassembled at point A, and fused together at point B.

Weeks passed, and Brundle was seemingly still unaffected by the transportation. As time passed and no new conditions surfaced, Brundle continued clinging to a belief that there was a relationship between his perception of time and the multiplication rate of any possible microscopic factors (the fly in the chamber). If weeks had gone by with no negative effect, then the answer to the 'Memorex' question must be *live*.

Relatively soon Brundle began to notice changes in his physical characteristics. Another important observation to make when considering this film is that the changes he noticed were not considered by Brundle to be negative. In fact, Brundle had more physical strength, increased vitality and dexterity. He concluded that his state of being was positive, and although he had not identified any specific factors that belonged to the equation, he made the obvious conclusion that a change had taken place when he went through the transporter.

Eventually, Brundle's physical makeup began to mutate, his face wrecked with strange tissues and sores; and his fingernails peeled away from his fingers with ease. Brundle's environment was breaking down—he was transforming into a human fly as a result of the fusion.

After research Brundle found the root cause of his modified physical state: the fly in the chamber. Brundle's physical body continued to deteriorate, and he realized that he must return to the scientific method, the same method he previously ignored, if he was ever to survive. He started with the problem: How to reduce the amount of fly in Brundle? One of the more important things to note in the film—his problem a question (how to) and a proposition stating the things to be done (reduce). Also important is to note that his problem was not: I am turning into a human fly. Yes, being a human fly is a problem using the definition 'a source of distress,' but according to this doctrine Brundle's body was in a negative state.

Yet another important observation is that because the scientific method was ignored during the life cycle of the environment, the application of a scientific method after the mutation was not sufficient to reverse the negative conditions. Again note Brundle's problem: How to reduce the amount of fly in Brundle? Brundle knew this rule when formulating his problem; there was no way to completely reverse the negative state—his best expectation was only to reduce the contributing negative factors to a manageable level.

Like the fly, event the most microscopic factors can wreck environments that are exponentially larger than the factor itself; often there is no relationship between the perceived size of any factor and the scope of the environment as a whole.

View the film to see the conclusion and draw the parallel between Brundle and any computing environment where the scientific method is ignored even briefly.

12

reducing negative potential

Negative potential is a weakness that has been identified but not exploited. This is usually determined by study of the map or analysis of the environment.

When measuring potential, if a networked system is somehow connected to a larger network such as the Internet, the potential for a negative state is in fact infinite or considering the limitations of time immeasurable.

An example of a negative potential: an errorless system that does not have an anti-virus subsystem. There may be no current virus threat, but without measures against viruses the potential for infection does exist. It is realistic to say that the system may never be subject to a virus infection depending on scope of use and other factors, but without protection an infection is within the realm of possibility; in other words, it has the potential of occurring.

Data security is another area where the potential for a negative state may always exist. Again, if a network is never infiltrated no negative state will ever surface as a result of an infiltration; but if the appropriate security precautions are not taken the potential will always exist. 'Hackers' often exploit this potential.

The following paragraphs present an example of *potential reduction* in an environment where an anti-virus subsystem does not exist but must be quickly implemented based on a virus event.

A user in a community of twenty thousand has executed an electronic mail attachment that has spawned malicious code. This self-replicating code, or virus, begins to replicate to file systems that are unprotected from anonymous entities (users or viruses). Twenty thousand interconnected workstations are unprotected from this threat. It is known by observation that at least one workstation is affected. Research on the properties of the virus indicates that it will replicate to shared file systems, verified by the presence of the virus file on said systems in the environment. Maps clearly indicate where shared file systems are located, and the quickest method of threat containment and potential reduction is obvious. Anti-virus subsystems are placed at these shared file systems, or the point of file exchange between users. Because the public areas are protected, the virus is removed before others can access it, or the virus' replication attempts are denied altogether by the file system hosting the anti-virus subsystem—the potential of the virus spreading to other workstations is greatly reduced.

To draw a parallel line between this example and a real-world scenario: If a single person is hosting a virus, if he does not leave his residence and does not come in contact with any other humans, the threat is greatly reduced. As soon as he enters a shopping mall or hops aboard a train (shared system), the threat grows exponentially. When there is such a threat in human worlds, transportation is restricted to and from certain locales. This is 'threat containment', or a quarantine process; in other words: a reduction in infection potential.

In the example, the potential for infection was reduced but it still exists. What was the source, or root cause, of the outbreak? In this example, a user executed an electronic mail attachment that started the event—could another user do the same? Is anti-virus protection needed at the mail gateways? Taking this action would again reduce potential. If the mail gateways and shared file systems are protected, is anti-virus software still required at the workstation? By implementing protection at the workstation, potential would be further reduced and so on.

After measures are taken to reduce potential, the new problem is: How is the effectiveness of any steps taken to reduce potential measured when no attempt to exploit the potential is taking place?

To continue with the previous example: After the virus event, the new anti-virus subsystems go for months without detecting another virus. Although services are active and logs indicate everything is running by design, how does the engineer know that if a virus is introduced the recently deployed anti-virus subsystems will prevent the spread of infection or, for that matter, that another virus does not already exist?

The solution to the problem is: Test the resistance of the solution.

In the case of the anti-virus subsystems, the introduction of a harmless virus string into the environment would allow for testing of the virus detection and alert mechanisms. Alternatively, a virus could be released into an isolated lab environment protected by alternative measures. Although many administrators might gasp at the thought of introducing a virus into a system, if they are gasping then perhaps they are retaining a false idea about what a virus really is. A virus is a program that can be the subject of study like any other program; subject to identification, magnification, isolation, and so on. A valid problem is—How can the computing environment be protected from viruses without using anti-virus software?

13

other factors

During research, the public network is often used as a reference point for viewing the tenants of other engineers, specialists, and consultants. The origin of software or procedures should be considered.

Just as any computing environment may benefit from the public network; it also is subject to the disadvantages of its use. Information, when unverified, can be dangerous. Alerts that originated from the public network have directed administrators and users to effect preventative measures for viruses that do not exist; preventative measures that actually damaged the productivity of individual computing environments and the world's computing environment as a whole. This has happened on more than one occasion on a frequency that was measurable, through mass media, even by those who had never touched a computer. During the twenty-first century, the saying 'Information is power' became quite popular—one should always remember that although some information has potential power; information is not actual power until applied and useless information can easily be disposed of.

Over a decade ago, a strain of the *Stoned* virus was making rounds in a computer store I where I worked. A quagmire of events led up to a high number of infections, which could have easily been prevented or reduced in number by simply write-protecting the floppy disks (potential reduction) used to boot systems for the purpose of running diagnostic routines and even anti-virus software. I walked into the store one day and noted that one technician had memory chips removed from the system board and spread on the bench. He claimed that the chips needed to 'lose their charge' to ensure the memory-resident segment of the virus was eliminated. At the time, removing several megabytes of memory from a system was not a quick task; done correctly it required a special tool to pry a multitude individual chips from their sockets. I remember wondering how long he planned to leave the chips lying on the bench, or how removing memory chips from a circuit board prevented the return of the virus.

This is an example of unnecessary reduction in potential. In fact, not only was this unnecessary, there was no sound reasoning behind the effort—the ideas were purely imaginative. In this example, nothing was reduced, because the memory-resident virus ceased to reside in the chips after power was removed from the system—the chips were not 'charged' and no instruction could be carried if the system was inoperable. This technician actually created more negative potential by removing the chips (potential of breaking a chip leg during the removal process or the chips being damaged by electrostatic discharge) than if he left them intact. The shop supervisor had a different opinion, however, wanting so badly to rid the shop of this rampant problem that he enforced the chip removal procedure as part of a standard for removing the virus.

The point is this: A computing environment may be directly influenced by expectations or ideas that are imaginary or not relevant. Not everyone with an interest in the computing environment is an engineer, such as the shop supervisor in the previous example. On a larger scale, computing environments can also be affected by industry temperature or current hysterias, and subject to changes based on rumors and new standards (invented by the media), which often are a child of said rumors. These standards, as they are passed through media outlets and the public network can become less scientific as they migrate; facts can be replaced by myths, and perceptions sometimes replace actual working designs.

There are two major types of human influences on computing environments: the members of proxy groups or those with the most imagined or conceptual perspective (the technician who influenced the shop supervisor in the previous example); and the architects and engineers, or those with the actual measurements. If engaged in a practice where a company, unit, or network is subject to measurement by the public or a large corporation, then unfortunately there must be some type of balance between the actual needs of the environment and the needs of the public.

For example, consider one administrator who updates all the computer systems in his environment with every known software update applicable to said systems. In this case, is it necessary to implement stop measures for vulnerabilities that will never surface or to enable features that will never be used?

Is it also possible that this administrator is introducing count-less flies, as they were described earlier in this writing, into the computing environment?

A second administrator analyzes every software update and after research and testing determines that only a few updates are required to maintain the environment as it is used, and also to reduce the negative potential where said potential has been detected by analysis. In this scenario, is there a possibility that other updates are still needed based on the expectations or requirements of other groups with an interest in the environment?

A third administrator does not make an effort to measure potential—is this administrator vulnerable to both technical and political damage?

The answer to all questions is yes. The problem becomes: How are both the technical and political needs of the computing environment satisfied?

In the eyes of the community, the first administrator provided a bulletproof computing environment, but left out several critical steps that have been discussed throughout this reference. In many cases, this does not mean that the engineers are not capable of these analyses, but that they have been influenced or pressured into bypassing methods that the engineers themselves know to be correct.

Technically speaking, the second administrator took the correct approach to reducing negative potential in the environment, without entertaining paranoia. However, there may be needs unmet by this approach, such as satisfying those with a low level of understanding who want measures against impossible scenarios implemented, regardless of technical merit or lack thereof.

A computing environment can be heavily influenced by outside factors: perceptions, feelings, and attitudes. The actual values of these factors, if they have the potential for negatively affecting the computing environment, can lead to a chain of events that can level a computing environment to the ground. These changes may not be immediately obvious, just like the case of Brundle and his fly, especially when considering a large operating environment and all of the components within.

14

investing in precision

Ever heard of 'rock climbing for speed'? It does exist, but the rock climber is generally interested in precision climbing and avoiding injury, not speed.

When faced with a climb, the initial grip may be that which the climber is most familiar with if he has climbed the rock before. If it is a new challenge, the most comfortable grip may be selected. Future moves are analyzed before execution. Each handhold or foothold is selected based on very specific properties, gathered through observation.

When rock climbers obtain a good position on a face, they pause and calculate the next move. Areas of the rock face are resistance tested before a grip is placed on them; some rocks may fall away or break apart when used as a handhold or foothold. Properties hidden from view (rock strength, integrity) are not assumed, but logically determined.

The climber's investment in the analysis of each component is returned when the climb is completed without error. The practice of precision continues to pay off, as the speed of determining the properties of the holds increases every time a rock is climbed, or with *experience*.

It must be stated that to properly engage in technically detailed tasks, one must first be properly motivated. A motive is the thing that causes a person to act. Therefore, to be in action motivation is required. In the case of the rock climber, it is the sense of accomplishment that is achieved when the climb is completed and the experience gained during the climb that motivates the climber.

There is a critical difference between enthusiasm and fear as motivators. Where fear is the motivator, no true work can take place. Common fears are: fear of losing a job; fear that political needs are not being met (this is usually the last consideration for the positively motivated/fearless specialist); fear of failure; fear that goals will be unmet.

When a rock is climbed because an angry bear is chasing the climber and the only desire of the climber is to escape—how efficient is this climb? Would this scramble up the rock face be used as an example for other rock climbers who wish to learn a tactical approach to rock climbing? If by chance the scramble was the most efficient climb, could the climber recall what climbing methods were utilized? Could that efficient climb be repeated?

Fear without an element of immediate danger, present in the relative safety of a computing environment, leads to procrastination. The unknown state is a breeding ground for fear. Any task can be intimidating and ultimately avoided if the thought of accomplishing it remains dark and the projection of success is a negative one. Procrastination can be brought on by the presence of negative/unknown factors that seem too numerous to measure.

If problems are approached as individual challenges and not as a perceived requirement for eliminating fear; if a positive motivator exists; then any problem can be solved—again, it is only a matter of using a tactical approach and gaining a true understanding using identification, magnification, and documentation. This gained understanding and experience is the reward, the motivator; the 'light bulb' goes on and so on.

What is so vastly complicated in a computing environment that it cannot be understood or assimilated? The answer is nothing—man invented it all. The current state of technology as a whole is the result of progression, of magnification, of differencing, and all the other fundamentals discussed here. The first computer was a small forward step from the abacus; a *simple* device. One can start with a stone and progressively understand the modern computing environment.

In some cases, the engineer will start with the stone. Starting with the stone only means more time will be needed to gain an understanding, as opposed to starting with an abacus, with Babbage's machine, the Timex Sinclair, the IBM PC, or a series of IBM PCs on a Token Ring network, and so on.

It is obvious that more time is required when starting with the stone. How are leaps made in this case where time is limited? What is the difference between the abacus and other systems? The comparison of properties and use of comparisons far exceeds a 'cold' method of exploration as an efficient use of time. Straight study of a modern workstation with no knowledge of relatively simpler types is a more complex study than a *progressive* study starting with something that is easily assimilated, such as the stone or the abacus. This principle of gaining understanding is the same as the magnification principle mentioned earlier in this reference—instead of analyzing a completed *diagram B*, trying to assimilate everything, start with *diagram A* and logically advance in understanding and knowledge.

Once understanding is achieved, time-efficient problem solving becomes a matter of focus. The specialist must formulate and solve problems in sequence. Task A, hours 1-5; task B, hours 6-9—*not* task A, hours 1, 3, 5, 7, 9 and task B, hours 2, 4, 6, 8; using the latter the focus is lost at points 1, 2, 3, 4, 5, 6, 7, 8 and 9 in time.

'Slicing' the time allocated for one specific task must be avoided whenever possible. Consider a person that is faced with the task of doing a full load of laundry and a sink full of dishes. There is a perceived immediate need for a clean pair of socks and a clean glass. Because an *immediate* need has been identified, does this warrant sabotaging the timely delivery of known future needs, like the availability of the rest of the clean laundry or utensils? How efficient would it be for the person to start the dishwasher (the scientific process) to wash only a single glass, or to start the washing machine with only a single pair of socks in it? Yes, the immediate need will be met: a clean pair of socks and clean glass; but the needs of the total environment have not been satisfied, and could be with a simple consolidation of tasks. The focus is on dishwashing—no laundry will be done during this time. Yes, it is faster to only put a single glass in the dishwasher and start the cycle, but with a small increase in time investment (loading the rest of the dishes) the future gain is great. If the next perceived need is a clean fork—that need is swiftly met.

In my practice, I have used the simpler analogy of a 'flushing toilet' to drive this point. I have stated that the details of work being done are like water in a toilet bowl, the toilet bowl being the human mind. When tasks are switched, the toilet is flushed and focus is lost. Of course the details return in a slow trickle, slow being the operative word, but having to reinvent or revisit some of those ideas is in fact double work. Relearning that which has already been learned is not an efficient use of time.

During any engineering effort, a certain amount of information remains in the mind until it can be transferred to a map or document. Although it has been suggested here that the map should reflect the environment directly, the environment cannot be mapped in real time. In the end all details should be clearly indicated on the final map, but until that point is reached, focus is the battery that powers the map in the mind. Once the end solution is reached, the toilet can be flushed and the focus shifted to another problem. This suggests that a completed map represents task completion and confirms that the creation of the map is also a portion of the work. It also suggests that if the map were created as close to real time as possible, this would be more efficient, provide resistance to detail loss, and allow quick restoration of focus by view of the map.

If the map was created *in parallel* with discovery and focus is lost, then details can be refreshed with minimal relearning. An added benefit of documentation in parallel with the main effort is that the map is complete (or near completion) when the task is complete. The main body of work and the record of what was done (already known to be an effort in itself) when separated allow detail loss. If no map exists after a solution has been implemented, all details must be rediscovered to create the map. Why separate this, when such a great opportunity exists for transferring these facts when they are close to the specialist? Returning to an analogy used in the beginning of these writings—remember the lost traveler? If the traveler records every move *at the time of each move* and covers a whole area, when he finds his way he will also have a completed map; and if asked for a map of the area, it is already done—there is no further work.

The difference between the amount of time it is 'imagined' a given task will take, and the actual amount of time to accomplish it is usually great; in some cases that difference is in favor of the engineer and in other cases against. The fact remains that the 'green cheese' must be placed—the grip must be obtained—to begin to eliminate the unknown areas where 'demotivators' begin to collect if no action is taken.

Sometimes specialists reserve large blocks of time for specific tasks based only on imaginative ideas of how long said task will take—procrastination may be an influence in these cases. Other times, in an effort to meet a goal or set precedent, the engineer or specialist does not reserve *enough* time to accomplish the task. If the goal is 'a perfect climb', then the proper amount of time must be allocated for perfection. This is one of the most common problems found in computer engineering and administration. The most important investment in any effort is enough time to absolutely solve the problem, document the solution, test the solution, implement the solution, resistance test the solution, and measure any negative potential.

What amount of time should be allocated? To answer this, an appraisal is required. If the engineer is armed with a library of time measurements for every task previously engaged then fact-based estimates will be available for future tasks that are the same or similar. Picture a simple notebook, with a task description and time required for every task that has already been executed—this would have a definite value for any engineer. As stated throughout this writing, measurement is always an intelligent investment—this also applies to time. In fact, in the case of time the actual process of measurement is automatic, one only needs to keep records. The payoff is exponential because imaginative influence is removed from estimates; if time is mapped, a factual idea of how long processes will take will be known and future time can be reserved accordingly.

Differencing covers ground by applying existing levels of understanding to like systems. Applied focus to a particular subsystem or problem equals greater education—an education that can be used in differencing and other forms of analysis. Consolidation or grouping of similar tasks, in addition to creating efficiency, confirms the similarities between technology types. Keeping as close to a real time record as possible during analysis and problem solving eliminates the need for relearning, including cyclically relearning how long repeating tasks take by engaging in the task again and again. A combination of all of these methods will provide a gain in available time, which can be invested in observation, more in-depth analysis, and refinement of the 'iconic' language as applied to maps; but if a positive motivator is not present these methods lose all potential. There must be a real interest in the goal of solving the problem.

15

the language of the map

In most administrative scenarios, maps created by the engineer or specialist will be shared with other individuals, both technical and nontechnical. It is known that the primary purpose of a map is to provide an accurate reflection of the environment for analysis and problem-solving purposes.

The map has a secondary purpose as a communications medium; but these communications are worthless if they can only be translated by the individual who drew the charts—destroying the value of the map as a means of communicating the details of the environment to others.

The art of map creation is where the author creates a reference that is both easily viewed (nontechnical audience) *and* accurately reflects the technology and the detail of said technology (technical audience). A balance between art and schematic must be achieved to accomplish the creation of this 'all-purpose' map.

Nontechnical parties sometimes prefer to be spared deep technical detail—but if technical details are presented in a way that is pleasing to the eye, then to a nontechnical individual this representation is more art than schematic. The technical map should be 'polished' when complete; crude representation of network equipment on the technically correct drawing should be replaced with representation that has artistic value. Data flows should be represented in an elegant and clean manner. Simple rearrangement of cables represented on a diagram (the same way that a neat arrangement should take place in a communications closet) can relieve the mind of the viewer, both technical and nontechnical alike.

Can a tangled web of twisted cables in a closet still facilitate network communications if the cables are all connected to the correct ports at the ends? Most certainly—I have seen this firsthand on several occasions. But when 'other interested parties' walk into that communications closet to obtain a behind-the-scenes 'picture' and struggle to obtain that basic picture of how devices are connected (because the cables are a tangled mess), confusion replaces clear understanding. In fact, without special equipment (such as a 'fox and hound') it is unlikely anyone that was not directly involved in establishing the twisted connections would have any clue what connectivity is in place and could probably not glean even a basic understanding of how it works.

On the opposite end of this spectrum, a *basic* understating (on which further levels of understanding are built) of inter-communications when viewing a neat cable arrangement (with proper color coding and labeling) is *automatic* by simple view. In fact, that view is immediately impressed on the mind and stays with the viewer. It is that type of 'first impression' that can be achieved by the artistically enhanced map.

Marketing organizations for software companies are often well practiced in this art—they wish to impress the technical merit of their software on nontechnical audiences as well as technical audiences—and often provide maps with specially arranged technical subject matter so they can be digested by anyone.

16

similar options

The benefits of computing standards are almost beyond measure. Use of differencing was discussed earlier, and using standard configurations will enhance the effectiveness of that differencing method exponentially. Every workstation or server system is an operational result of the hardware and software *options* that have been enabled to achieve a working system—a system that meets the requirements of the tasks at hand.

The potential of one setting having an effect on the whole subsystem or the entire system is known. In an optimal configuration, a single, *perfected* set of options should be known and applied where the requirements are the same.

If a *single* set of parameters, in both the areas of hardware and software, is chosen based on careful determination and experiment and the exact parameters are 'cloned' across all workstations, all users will have the same computing experience (where input is the same). Only when one or more of those parameters are modified will the computer provide a different result—at that point the user with the dissimilar experience is known to be working with other factors.

A need for exclusive operating environments will sometimes be perceived. Users will often take the position that their work is unique and that exceptions to standards are required. However, the need/importance of these unique requirements must be measured. The weight or value of standards is usually greater than the special requirement. The question must be asked: How can one user's special needs be incorporated into the standard, allowing continued use of a single set of options?

A unique subsystem requires additional documentation—where standards can be achieved, time spent both in administration and documentation is saved. There is also a problem solving benefit: if there are fewer factors, the equation is simply less complicated.

Where a unique requirement is proposed and that need has been determined to be valid, the possibility of modifying the overall standard to meet the unique requirement (as opposed to integrating a unique system with the other standard systems) should *always* be explored. Consider this problem: Can unique requirements be satisfied by modifying standard options, even though such modifications would only be beneficial (from the user's perspective) to a single user type? If enabling the options to meet these requirements does not affect the output of the other common/standard configurations, then the answer is generally yes. Although the benefit may not be apparent to the common users, the administrative benefits are again exponential.

Have you ever purchased a vehicle with only the standard options? Sitting in this vehicle, you may note that there are spaces reserved in the dashboard for the options you did not select, such as the controls to adjust seat temperature. A 'dummy' button or plate may fill the space where the controls would exist had you selected the heated seat option in the car.

Although the plates that fill these spaces may not be visually pleasing, they do not affect the functionality of the options you *did* select. This is an example where a single standard is in place that accommodates all users—there is one design for the dashboard that can be used by all. It would be extremely inefficient for engineers to design a separate dashboard for every set of options. The 'incomplete' looking dashboard is the sacrifice in this scenario. The reduction in overhead that is gained by having one single design and implementation procedure (which involves engineering, programming, robotics, etc.) far outweighs the impact of having a dashboard that may look incomplete to some.

17

seven notes

The guitar in one common configuration is a six-stringed instrument. How does the six-string guitar sound when a chord is played and one string is out of tune? This out of tune string can be the result of strumming, or *regular use* of the instrument. When a guitar is out of tune, this does not mean that the design of the guitar is flawed. The potential for the guitar needing tuning during regular use is *known* and there is no problem, such as: Why is the guitar out of tune?

What each string should sound is also known, by default: the notes *E A D G B E*. The guitar player knows these musical values, and because of this knowledge the settings can be restored by tuning. The more times the tuning procedure takes place the easier it becomes. The first hundred or so times the guitar is tuned the musician may use an electronic tuning device. As experience is gained, the musician may be trained enough to tune the device without using the electronic tuner at all. After tuning the instrument five hundred times, the musician may begin to recognize how frequently the guitar is being adjusted. If the instrument needs to be adjusted more often than usual, as determined by observation, it would be obvious to the musician that some other factor is present such as extreme temperature change or worn strings.

When not facing technical challenges, I sometimes pick up a guitar. When I first started to play, the first thing I attempted was to learn one single chord. The problem was how to arrange my fingers to play this chord. Eventually, I researched and solved the problem and was able to play that single chord.

My interest in the instrument grew. One evening I was talking to a musician in a local bar, and got an interesting response to a question. I asked him "How difficult is it to master the guitar?" and his words, which I often recall both when playing the guitar and when facing technical challenges was:

"Not difficult. Seven notes. That's it—that's all you have to know. Everything else comes from those seven notes."

His statement directly supported the idea that a system immediately perceived as complicated is nothing more than an assembly of simple elements. The perception of complexity originates from the assembly itself or how the options are combined into a system. The elements by themselves are not unique; it is their relationships and their arrangement that create a unique whole.

978-0-595-37670-4
0-595-37670-3